D1127991

TIMELINES OF
AMERICAN HISTORY ™

A Timeline of the
First Continental Congress

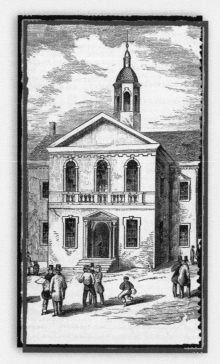

Maxine Rosaler

rosen
central ™

The Rosen Publishing Group, Inc., New York

Published in 2004 by The Rosen Publishing Group, Inc.
29 East 21st Street, New York, NY 10010

Library of Congress Cataloging-in-Publication Data

Rosaler, Maxine.
A timeline of the First Continental Congress / Maxine Rosaler.—1st ed.
    p. cm.—(Timelines of American history)
Summary: Provides a chronological look at the history of the American colonies when their leaders were struggling with decisions about whether rebellion was right response to the tyranny of Great Britain.
Includes bibliographical references (p.) and index.
ISBN 0-8239-4545-6 (lib. bdg.)
1. United States. Continental Congress—History—Chronology—Juvenile literature. 2. United States—Politics and government—To 1775—Chronology—Juvenile literature. [1. United States. Continental Congress—History—Chronology. 2. United States—Politics and government—1775–1783—Chronology.] I. Title. II. Series.
E303.R67 2004
973.3'12'0202—dc22

                                                        2003015544

Manufactured in the United States of America

On the cover: This painting by Clyde D. De Land shows Patrick Henry, one of Massachusetts' delegates to the First Continental Congress, delivering a speech.
On the title page: This is an illustration depicting Carpenters' Hall in Philadelphia, Pennsylvania, site of the First Continental Congress in September and October of 1774.

Contents

1

British Tyranny and Colonial Anger

The French and Indian War waged in North America was won by Great Britain in 1763. British and American soldiers had fought side by side as brothers, defeating the French and their Indian allies. This spirit of brotherhood and cooperation would not last long, however. Immediately after the war, British prime minister George Grenville began to try to control the colonies more and raise money by taxing them. This new policy would eventually lead to the creation of the First Continental Congress and colonial rebellion.

British prime minister George Grenville tried to control the American colonies by taxing them. Instead, his policies helped bring about a revolution.

May 1756

War is declared between the French and British. The French and Indian War is waged from the Ohio and Hudson Valleys, north to Detroit, Michigan, and the provinces of Ontario, Quebec, and Nova Scotia in Canada.

February 10, 1763

The Treaty of Paris is signed, ending the French and Indian War. With the help of American colonists, Great Britain has seized control of Canada and the lands along the length of the Mississippi River (except for New Orleans) from the French.

This 1755 painting depicts a battle in the French and Indian War. British soldiers and their American supporters can be seen firing on and attacking the French and their Indian allies.

April 1763

George Grenville becomes prime minister of England. In order to pay off some of England's debts, Grenville begins to impose a series of taxes on the American colonies.

April 5, 1764

The Sugar Act, which charges colonists taxes on molasses and sugar, is passed into law by Parliament. The bill had been introduced by Lord Grenville.

Unpopular Acts of Parliament

The Sugar Act was followed by a series of other acts that placed taxes on the American colonists or limited their freedom. In 1764, the Currency Act was passed, forbidding the colonies from issuing their own currency (money). Two more unpopular acts were passed in 1765—the Quartering Act and the Stamp Act. The Quartering Act forced colonists to house, supply, and feed the British troops stationed in the colonies. The Stamp Act taxed newspapers, pamphlets, legal documents, playing cards, and other kinds of printed paper.

ADVERTISEMENT.

THE Members of the Association of the Sons of Liberty, are requested to meet at the City-Hall, at one o'Clock, To-morrow, (being Friday) on Business of the utmost Importance ;—And every other Friend to the Liberties, and Trade of America, are hereby most cordially invited, to meet at the same Time and Place.   *The Committee of the Association.*

Thursday, NEW-YORK, 16th December, 1773.

This 1773 advertisement announces a meeting in New York's City Hall of the local chapter of the Sons of Liberty, a secret organization of colonists opposed to the Stamp Act.

★ **September 1, 1764**

The Currency Act is passed, forbidding American colonies from issuing their own currency. This act allows Great Britain to regain control over the colonies' currency system.

★ **Late 1764**

Massachusetts colonists, angered by the Sugar Act and Currency Act, suggest a unified protest involving all thirteen colonies. As a result, many of the colonies stop importing English goods.

An angry Boston mob protests the Stamp Act by throwing stamped papers into a bonfire in 1765.

★ **March 22, 1765**

Parliament passes the Stamp Act. The act gains its name because printed materials are stamped once the tax is paid on them.

★ **Summer 1765**

A network of secret organizations called the Sons of Liberty is created throughout the colonies. Its members try to threaten with violence the stamp agents who collect Stamp Act taxes. Many stamp agents quit, and the tax is repealed (cancelled) in 1766.

7

Colonial Committees of Correspondence

Though the Stamp Act was repealed, Parliament quickly issued a Declaratory Act, stating that it had the right to tax the colonies whenever and in whatever way it wished. The colonists' distrust of England grew. Committees of Correspondence were created so that colonists could share ideas on how to resist England's growing attempts to control the colonies. The committees conducted town meetings throughout the thirteen colonies and communicated with each other by letter. Massachusetts Bay was the most radical American colony. One of its members—Samuel Adams—drew up a document called the Rights of the Colonists: colonists had the right to life, liberty, and property without interference from England. The committees' protests against English policy would lead directly to the creation of the First Continental Congress a few years later.

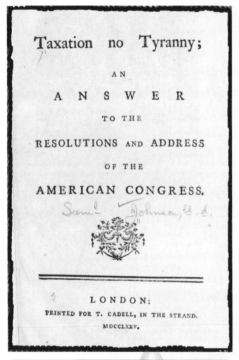

The British paid close attention to the tax protests in the American colonies. This 1775 British pamphlet is a response to demands for colonial rights.

November 2, 1772
At a Boston town meeting, Samuel Adams proposes that a network of "corresponding societies" be established in Massachusetts.

November 1772
The Boston Committee of Correspondence is created. Committees from nine surrounding towns participate. The Boston Committee urges all thirteen colonies to stop importing British goods.

Samuel Adams

March 1773
The Virginia House of Burgesses—the representative government of the colony of Virginia—sends out a request to the other colonies, urging them to follow Massachusetts Bay's example.

March 1774
By this time, all the colonies except Pennsylvania have established Committees of Correspondence.

2
The Continental Congress Is Born

In 1773, England again angered the colonists by forcing them to buy their tea from only one supplier—the East India Company—leading to an increase in tea prices. On December 16, 1773, 150 Bostonians dressed as Mohawk Indians threw 90,000 pounds (40,823.3 kilograms) of East India Company tea into Boston Harbor. In response, Parliament passed a bill called the Coercive Acts. In addition to closing Boston Harbor until the colonists paid for the

Dressed as Indians, a group of Bostonians board a British ship and throw its crates into Boston Harbor to protest the Tea Act and taxes on tea. The Boston Tea Party took place on December 17, 1773.

destroyed tea, the acts also gave the British governor almost complete control over the Massachusetts Bay Colony.

★ **May 1773**
Parliament passes the Tea Act, which forces the colonies to buy tea only from the East India Company. Together with a tea tax, this makes tea more expensive.

★ **September 27, 1773**
Samuel Adams, writing in the *Boston Gazette*, proposes that a "Congress of the American States" be assembled as soon as possible to draw up a bill of rights.

★ **December 16, 1773**
About 150 Bostonians dressed as Indians board three ships carrying East India Company tea and throw the cargo into the harbor. This protest becomes known as the Boston Tea Party.

★ **May 1774**
Paul Revere rides from Boston to Philadelphia, warning colonists of an English blockade of Boston Harbor and urging unified colonial opposition.

Paul Revere warns colonists of a coming British attack.

The Intolerable Acts and the Gathering of a Congress

The British Parliament responded to the Boston Tea Party by passing several laws known as the Coercive Acts. To coerce someone is to

THE

PETITION

OF THE

GRAND AMERICAN CONTINENTAL

CONGRESS,

TO THE

KING's

Moft Excellent Majefty.

AMERICA:

BOSTON, Printed and fold at the Printing-Office, near the MILL-BRIDGE.

The First Continental Congress gathered in the autumn of 1774 to agree on a list of demands for greater colonial rights. The petition to King George III that resulted from the Congress's meetings is shown above.

try to force him or her to do what you want the person to do. In the colonies, the laws were called the Intolerable Acts. When something is intolerable, it is something that you cannot stand to live with. Several Committees of Correspondence called for a convention of colonial delegates to organize resistance to the acts. This convention was the First Continental Congress, held in Philadelphia in the early fall of 1774.

★ March 1774–June 1774

A series of laws are passed that become known as the Coercive Acts. The colonists refer to them as the Intolerable Acts. They are designed to force the American colonies to submit to Britain's control.

★ June 1774

Connecticut becomes one of the first colonies to choose delegates for the First Continental Congress.

★ August 1774

The British governor of Georgia prevents delegates of the colony from attending the First Continental Congress.

★ August 19, 1774

Massachusetts's four delegates—including John Adams and his cousin Samuel Adams—leave Boston for Philadelphia to attend the Continental Congress.

★ Late August 1774

Fifty-five delegates from twelve colonies arrive in Philadelphia and prepare for the Congress.

Carpenters' Hall, the site of the First Continental Congress

The First Continental Congress Begins Its Work

The First Continental Congress began its first official meeting on September 5, 1774, in Philadelphia's Carpenters' Hall. Some of the most important delegates included George Washington and Patrick Henry from Virginia and John Adams and Samuel Adams from Massachusetts. Peyton Randolph of Virginia was chosen as the Congress's president. He had a reputation as a moderate due to his calm opposition to the British Parliament. Randolph seemed to occupy a good middle ground between the more conservative delegates, who wanted to make peace with Britain, and the more radical representatives, who were interested in gaining independence.

The First Continental Congress begins its work on September 5, 1774, in Philadelphia's Carpenters' Hall.

Late August 1774

Delegates from the twelve colonies meet each other and share their views before the Congress begins.

Charles Thompson

Early September 1774

Charles Thompson of Philadelphia, a radical, is nominated as permanent secretary of the Congress. Peyton Randolph, a moderate, is nominated as president.

September 5, 1774

The First Continental Congress begins. All delegates express support for the Congress's aim of presenting a united front against Britain's colonial policies.

September 6, 1774

Delegates agree on how the Congress will operate. They decide that each colony will have one vote and delegates must not speak to the press. A committee is formed to define the rights of the colonies and explain how Britain had ignored them.

3

Taking a Hard Line

The delegates to the First Continental Congress were affected by the mood of Philadelphia's residents. This already angry mood became even more anti-British on September 6, 1774. On that day, frightening news arrived from Boston. A rumor, known as the Powder Alarm, had spread, claiming that British general Thomas Gage was preparing to attack Boston. The Powder Alarm made the delegates angrier at the British, making it easier for the more anti-British delegates to win over to their side the more cautious colonial representatives.

The first days of the Continental Congress were spent choosing leaders, deciding on procedures, forming committees, and reacting to the frightening rumors of the Powder Alarm.

★ Early September 1774

British soldiers under General Thomas Gage seize Boston militia gunpowder stored in Cambridge, Massachusetts.

★ September 6, 1774

The Continental Congress and the city of Philadelphia receive an inaccurate report called the Powder Alarm. The report says that General Gage has ordered the warships in Boston Harbor to begin shelling the city. Both the delegates and Philadelphia residents are shocked and angered.

★ September 8, 1774

A second more accurate report arrives in Philadelphia. It states that General Gage is making preparations for war but has not yet ordered his warships to fire on Boston.

Thomas Gage

★ Mid-September 1774

The Continental Congress's committees discuss colonial rights, British tyranny, and the effects of taxation and the Intolerable Acts on the colonial economy.

The Suffolk Resolves

While the committees of the First Continental Congress were debating colonial rights and British tyranny, Boston-area colonists were also busy discussing these issues. In a congress held in Suffolk County, the Bostonians drew up a document known as the Suffolk Resolves. In it, they declared that the Intolerable Acts were illegal and should be disobeyed. They called for the creation of a colonial government that would raise its own taxes and a militia that would protect colonists from British aggression. Finally, the Suffolk Resolves urged merchants to stop trading with Britain. Paul Revere delivered a copy of this document to the Continental Congress on September 16, 1774. The Suffolk Resolves quickly divided the Congress into loyalist and revolutionary camps.

★ **September 9, 1774**
A Boston-area congress held in Suffolk County draws up the Suffolk Resolves. This document pledges disobedience to Britain's Intolerable Acts.

★ **September 16, 1774**
Paul Revere rides into Philadelphia with a copy of the Suffolk Resolves. The document is delivered to the Continental Congress delegates.

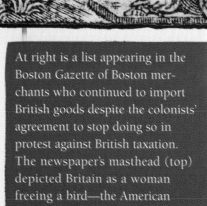

A LIST of the Names of *those*
who AUDACIOUSLY continue to counteract the UNIT-
ED SENTIMENTS of the BODY of Merchants thro'out
NORTH-AMERICA ; by importing British Goods
contrary to the Agreement.

John Bernard,
    (In King-Street, almost opposite Vernon's Head.
James McMasters,
             (On Treat's Wharf.
Patrick McMasters,
          (Opposite the Sign of the Lamb.
John Mein,
    (Opposite the White-Horse, and in King-Street.
Ame & Elizabeth Cummings,
  (Opposite the Old Brick Meeting House, all of Boston.
And, *Henry Barnes,*

At right is a list appearing in the Boston Gazette of Boston merchants who continued to import British goods despite the colonists' agreement to stop doing so in protest against British taxation. The newspaper's masthead (top) depicted Britain as a woman freeing a bird—the American colonies—from its cage.

★ September 17, 1774

The Continental Congress votes to support the Boston colonists and their Suffolk Resolves.

★ September 22, 1774

The Continental Congress asks all merchants of the colonies to stop importing British goods until the Congress decides how to protect colonial liberty against British aggression.

Loyalists Versus Revolutionaries

The First Continental Congress was split between loyalists and revolutionaries. Loyalists wished to remain loyal subjects of the king. Revolutionaries wished to break free of Britain's control and gain freedom to govern themselves without interference. The most powerful loyalist in the congress was Joseph Galloway. Fearing war with Britain, he proposed a Plan of Union. This plan would create an American Grand Council to make decisions together with the British Parliament on colonial matters.

★ **September 28, 1774**
Joseph Galloway proposes his Plan of Union. The Continental Congress spends the day debating it and votes to send the plan to a committee for further study.

★ **September 29, 1774**
The Boston Committee of Correspondence writes to the Continental Congress describing the sufferings of Boston citizens at the hands of the British army.

★ **Late September 1774**
South Carolina delegate Christopher Gadsen responds to rumors of a coming British attack with the words, "If [our towns] are burned down, we can rebuild them. But liberty once lost is gone forever."

20

This is a printed version of the proceedings of the First Continental Congress, containing the delegates' debates and decisions. It was printed in Philadelphia in 1774.

JOURNAL

OF THE

PROCEEDINGS

OF THE

CONGRESS,

Held at PHILADELPHIA,

September 5, 1774.

PHILADELPHIA:

Printed by WILLIAM and THOMAS BRADFORD, at the London Coffee-House.

DCC,LXXIV.

★ **Early October 1774**
George Washington writes to a friend in the British army, warning him of the consequences of British stubbornness, "[M]ore blood will be spilled . . . than history has ever furnished instances of in the annals of North America."

4

The First Continental Congress Vows to Fight Tyranny

B y the middle of October 1774, inspired by the fiery spirit of the Suffolk Resolves, the Continental Congress was ready to make a series of important decisions. Within a single week, the Congress agreed on a strong declaration of rights, took action to start a boycott of British goods, and rejected Joseph Galloway's compromise Plan of Union. By agreeing to this course of action, the colonies were agreeing that they would stand together with Boston against the British Parliament and its mighty army.

★ **October 14, 1774**
The Continental Congress agrees on a document called the Declaration and Resolves. It rejects the Intolerable Acts and claims that only the colonies have the right to make laws that affect the lives, liberty, and property of the colonists.

★ **October 18, 1774**
The Continental Congress adopts the Continental Association, an agreement that will put into effect a ban on all British imports by December 1, 1774.

Patrick Henry (*standing*) represented Virginia in the First Continental Congress. During this time he said, " I am not a Virginian, but an American!"

October 22, 1774 ★

The Continental Congress rejects Joseph Galloway's Plan of Union. The revolutionary delegates win out over the loyalists, and the congress stands firmly opposed to Britain.

October 26, 1774 ★

The Continental Congress writes to Quebec, asking it to stand united with the American colonies. A second letter is sent to King George III, stating the Congress's final decisions.

The United Colonies

On October 26, 1774, the First Continental Congress adjourned (came to an end). It agreed to meet again in the spring of 1775 if Britain had not done enough to address the colonies' complaints. A banquet was held at Philadelphia's City Tavern. Five hundred guests

toasted each other. A toast was even raised to King George III. The Congress had delivered a strong statement of defiance to the king and his Parliament, one that could lead to war. Some delegates thought war was certain, while others felt the British would back down. Whatever the outcome, the First Continental Congress had set a course for liberty.

Though he had greatly angered them, King George III (*above*) was toasted by the Continental Congress delegates and 500 guests during a banquet following the Congress's final day of work.

★ October 26, 1774
The First Continental Congress adjourns with the understanding that a second congress would gather in May 1775 if Britain continued to ignore the colonies' demands.

★ Fall 1774
John Adams expresses his belief that the Continental Congress's agreements and declarations will unify the colonies but "would be but waste paper in England."

★ December 1, 1774
Under the terms of the Continental Association, the colonies stop importing British goods. Under the same agreement, exports to Britain will stop by September 11, 1775, if Britain does not satisfy the colonists' demands.

John Adams

★ Late 1774
British troops fortify Boston and seize colonial ammunition, as local militiamen prepare for a fight with the king's army. Massachusetts Bay militiamen, known as minutemen, are organized for rapid response to British attacks.

The Road to War

The First Continental Congress had taken the strongest possible stand against Britain. Now King George III and Parliament would either have to back down or declare war on their own colonists. Though it did not declare independence from Britain, the Continental Congress did move the colonies much further down the road to liberty. The Congress also united the colonies in a single purpose and course of action. Just by gathering together leaders from the individual colonies, the Congress began to create an independent American government. Though the road that lay ahead was long and bloody, the First Continental Congress had laid the foundation for the United States of America.

This is the first page of the Olive Branch Petition sent by the First Continental Congress to King George III. In it, the delegates list their complaints against Britain and their demands for colonial rights. The petition also seeks a peaceful, friendly end to the colonial crisis..

⭐ **April 19, 1775**
British soldiers fight armed colonists at Lexington and Concord in Massachusetts. The first shots of the American Revolution are fired.

⭐ **May 10, 1775**
The Second Continental Congress meets in Philadelphia. Its main task is directing the war against the British.

⭐ **June 15, 1775**
George Washington is nominated to command the Continental army. He accepts the nomination the next day.

This is the document issued by the Continental Congress in June 1775 naming George Washington as "General and Commander in Chief of the army of the United Colonies."

July 4, 1776 The congress ratifies (accepts) Thomas Jefferson's Declaration of Independence. The colonies declare themselves to be states free and independent of Britain and united together as one nation.

27

A Timeline Mapping the Road to War

A timeline shows the most important events of a historical period and the dates on which those events occurred. The events are listed chronologically, meaning that they are listed in the order in which they happened. The earliest events come first, while the later events follow. The whole story of a historical period is not told in a timeline. Only basic facts are listed. Timelines offer a good way to get a quick idea of what happened during a certain period of time and how all the events fit together. Timelines help us see how one event causes later events. For example, we can see how the Boston Tea Party led to the passing of the Intolerable Acts, which then led to the meeting of the First Continental Congress and the setting of the colonies on the road to war with Britain.

Glossary

act (AKT) A law passed by a law-making body, such as Parliament or Congress.

bill (BIL) A proposal for action which may be voted on by a law-making body.

conservative (kun-SER-vuh-tiv) Someone who is in favor of slow change in politics and society or who is against any change at all.

declaration (deh-kluh-RAY-shun) An official statement of principles.

delegate (DEH-li-get) A person chosen by a group to represent them at a meeting.

George III (JORDGE the THURD) The king of Great Britain during the time of the American Revolution.

Intolerable Acts (in-TOL-ruh-bul AKTS) A series of laws passed by the British Parliament to punish the colony of Massachusetts after the Boston Tea Party. Also known as the Coercive Acts.

Parliament (PAR-lih-mint) The British legislature; the part of the government that passes laws in Great Britain.

radical (RAH-dih-kul) Someone who is in favor of big, quick changes in politics and society.

repeal (rih-PEEL) To take back, or cancel, a law.

Suffolk Resolves (SUH-foak rih-ZOLVS) A series of political statements written by Boston-area colonists that called for a tough stand against British tyranny.

tyranny (TEER-uh-nee) The unfair use of excessive power.

Web Sites

Due to the changing nature of Internet links, the Rosen Publishing Group, Inc., has developed an online list of Web sites related to the subject of this book. This site is updated regularly. Please use this link to access the list:

http://www.rosenlinks.com/tah/ficc

Index

Credits

About the Author: Maxine Rosaler is a freelance writer who lives in New York City.

ence
ip
y

Independence
Township
Library

chigan

Clarkston, Michigan

ndependence
Township
Library

Indepen
Town:
Libra

Clarkston, Michigan

Clarkston,

About the Author

Khrys Robinson is not your typical middle aged black woman. She has been working with children of all ages for over 20 years and has spent the last 12+ years traveling the world as a nanny. She currently resides in Brooklyn NY and uses her free time to create stories, run insane obstacle course races and dream of having a Sheepadoodle named Roscoe.

The End

And that is how Bella got her school picture with her super socks.

3-2-1...

Right as the picture snapped Bella threw her arms and legs in the air and smiled her

biggest and best smile.

Bella had to think fast.

The photographer smiled and said "No I'm sorry. It's just your face in the picture."

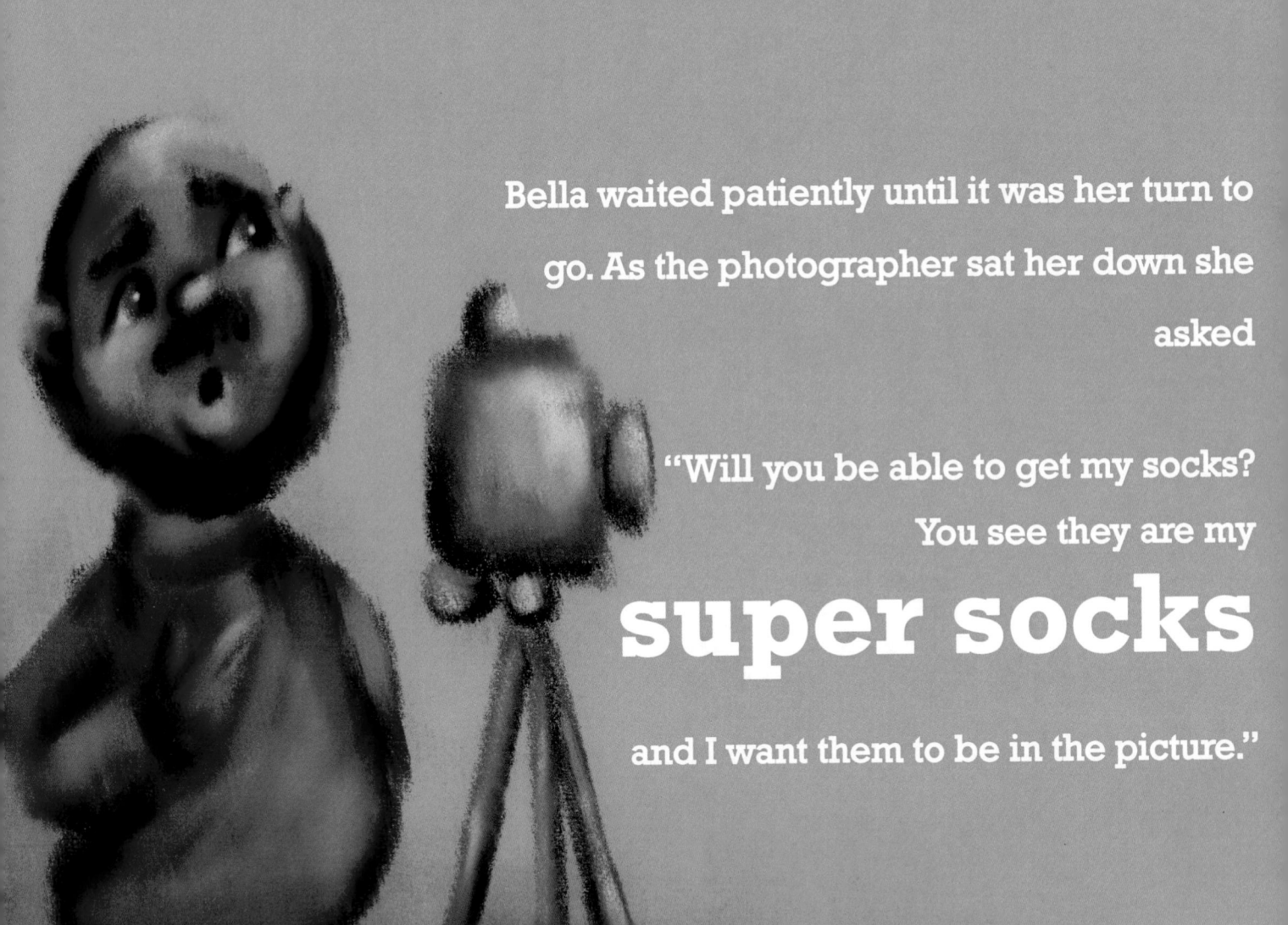

Bella waited patiently until it was her turn to go. As the photographer sat her down she asked

"Will you be able to get my socks? You see they are my

super socks

and I want them to be in the picture."

As everyone lined up to have their picture taken Bella got a brilliant idea.

Bella is stunned

"What? They won't show my socks?
Well we will just have to see about that." She says in a huff.

When Bella gets to school, she is excited to show her best friend Marley her special, purple, sparkly socks.

"Look Marley aren't they **pretty**? Mom let me wear them just for picture day."

Marley says "Oh yes. But Bella I do not think they will take a picture of your socks."

Bella stomps after her mom upstairs to change her outfit. After a minute her mom says "Why don't you wear your denim jumper? That way you can keep your green shirt on."

"Can I keep my purple sparkly socks and orange sneakers???"

"If you must"

"WOOHOO!!"

Bella changes out of her tutu and into her jumper.

Bella smiles with pride and says "It's picture day and this is my most perfect outfit. **LOOK I have on my magic socks!!**"

Bella's mom shakes her head "Honey your tutu is for playing at home, not for school."

Bella crosses her arms over her chest and **stomps** her foot. "But it's picture day and I want to look my best for kindergarten!"

"Let's go see what else we can find ok?"

"MOMMY IM READY!"

she sings as she twirls here and there

Bella's mom looks up from preparing breakfast.

"Oh Bella honey what is this?"

Bella takes her time finding the most perfect of perfect outfits.

"Hmmm I know!!!! I can wear my blue fluffy fluffy skirt with my favorite green shirt." *She claps her hands with glee.*

"Oh yes yes I will be the best."

Bella puts on her best outfit with her sparkly purple socks that come all the way to her knees, and her orange sneakers. She puts her favorite yellow ribbons in her hair and goes downstairs to show her mom.

Today is picture day so Bella has to look her very best, and must have the most perfect socks ever.

"Hmmm what socks should I wear? Do I want dots or maybe I should wear purple.

OOH I know! I can wear my purple sparkly socks!

Yes yes I will wear purple sparkly socks!" Bella giggles and skips to her closet to find the very best outfit to match her purple sparkly socks.

Some have sparkles like fairy dust.

Some have stripes like a zebra.

Some have dots like a lady bug.

Some socks have many colors and others are just plain.

Some socks come all the way up to her knees and others just to the ankle.

What are super socks??

Oh Bella has lots because she considers all of her socks

super duper.

Hi this is Bella.

Today is a special day because its picture day, and she gets to wear her **super socks.**

Letter from the Author:

When I created this character, I wanted to showcase the tiny version of myself. I was this little ball of amazing energy but I was extremely shy so I always kept it hidden. I wanted to write about a little girl having the confidence and fearlessness that I never knew I had. I believe every child has something about them that makes them simply amazing. I hope that Bella inspires every child that opens those pages to be their unique individual selves.

This is dedicated to two of the greatest uncles to ever walk the Earth. Uncle Jeff and Uncle Allon, you two were everything to me. You stayed with me every step of the way. Even though you weren't here physically, you always made your presence known for that extra little encouragement. Khrystal Rhea Khrys is finally doing it and this is all for you. Love you to the moon and back forever and always

Bella

and the

Great Picture Day

By Khrys Robinson
Illustrated by Stephanie Hider